Thanks for buying our book!

For a free
printable, email
paperpeonypress@gmail.com

and we will send
something fun to
your inbox!

for the love of books

PAPER PEONY PRESS

PAPER PEONY

book club

We love seeing all the books you're reading
and how you're keeping track of all those
great reads! Post on social media with hastag
#paperpeonybookclub
and can join our growing community of book lovers!

For the Love of Books for Kids
© Paper Peony Press.
First Edition, 2023

Published by: Paper Peony Press
@paperpeonypress
www.paperpeonypress.com

For wholesale inquiries contact: reagan@paperpeonypress.com

Printed in China

978-1-952842-97-9

this journal belongs to:

est
2022

TABLE OF
Contents

About Me

Name:

I am _____ years old.

I am in _____ grade.

My favorite place to read is...

- [ ] IN MY ROOM
- [ ] AT SCHOOL
- [ ] IN MY ROOM

- [ ] AT THE LIBRARY
- [ ]
- [ ]

My favorite types of books are:

- [ ] FAIRY TALES
- [ ] MYSTERY
- [ ] ADVENTURES
- [ ] NATURE
- [ ] COMIC BOOKS

- [ ] BIOGRAPHY
- [ ] HISTORY
- [ ]
- [ ]
- [ ]

Daily Reading Tracker

Check off the box for each day of the year that you read!

	1	2	3	4	5	6	7	8	9	10	11	12	13	14	15
Jan.	☐	☐	☐	☐	☐	☐	☐	☐	☐	☐	☐	☐	☐	☐	☐
Feb.	☐	☐	☐	☐	☐	☐	☐	☐	☐	☐	☐	☐	☐	☐	☐
Mar.	☐	☐	☐	☐	☐	☐	☐	☐	☐	☐	☐	☐	☐	☐	☐
April	☐	☐	☐	☐	☐	☐	☐	☐	☐	☐	☐	☐	☐	☐	☐
May	☐	☐	☐	☐	☐	☐	☐	☐	☐	☐	☐	☐	☐	☐	☐
June	☐	☐	☐	☐	☐	☐	☐	☐	☐	☐	☐	☐	☐	☐	☐
July	☐	☐	☐	☐	☐	☐	☐	☐	☐	☐	☐	☐	☐	☐	☐
Aug.	☐	☐	☐	☐	☐	☐	☐	☐	☐	☐	☐	☐	☐	☐	☐
Sept.	☐	☐	☐	☐	☐	☐	☐	☐	☐	☐	☐	☐	☐	☐	☐
Oct.	☐	☐	☐	☐	☐	☐	☐	☐	☐	☐	☐	☐	☐	☐	☐
Nov.	☐	☐	☐	☐	☐	☐	☐	☐	☐	☐	☐	☐	☐	☐	☐
Dec.	☐	☐	☐	☐	☐	☐	☐	☐	☐	☐	☐	☐	☐	☐	☐

YEAR: _____

16	17	18	19	20	21	22	23	24	25	26	27	28	29	30	31

BOOKS TO READ

Fill in the titles of books you want to read!

TITLE	AUTHOR	READ IT!

TITLE	AUTHOR	READ IT!
		■
		■
		■
		■
		■
		■
		■
		■
		■
		■
		■
		■
		■
		■
		■
		■
		■

TITLE	AUTHOR	READ IT!

Library Loans

✓	TITLE	DUE DATE
☐		/ /
		/ /
☐		/ /
		/ /
☐		/ /
		/ /
☐		/ /
		/ /
☐		/ /
		/ /
☐		/ /
		/ /
☐		/ /
		/ /
☐		/ /
		/ /
☐		/ /
		/ /
☐		/ /
		/ /
☐		/ /

Keep track of your library books and when they are due!
Check the box once your book is returned.

✓	TITLE	DUE DATE
☐		/ /
		/ /
☐		/ /
		/ /
☐		/ /
		/ /
☐		/ /
		/ /
☐		/ /
		/ /
☐		/ /
		/ /
☐		/ /
		/ /
☐		/ /
		/ /
☐		/ /
		/ /
☐		/ /

Book Review

BOOK #

audiobook ○
paperback ○
eBook ○

_____
TITLE

_____
AUTHOR

DATE   /   /

RATING ☆ ☆ ☆ ☆ ☆

LENGTH
_____
# of pages

○ NON-FICTION
○ FICTION

I LIKED THE ENDING
⊏ YES ⊐   /   ⊏ NO ⊐

I READ THIS BOOK

☐ by myself

☐ with: _____

FAVORITE CHARACTER

FAVORITE QUOTES

"
_____

_____

_____

_____

_____

_____ "

DRAW YOUR FAVORITE CHARACTER OR SCENE

I WOULD LIKE TO ASK THE AUTHOR...

_____

_____

_____

WOULD RECOMMEND TO A FRIEND? ⊏ YES ⊐ / ⊏ NO ⊐

Book Review

BOOK #

audiobook ○
paperback ○
eBook ○

_____
TITLE

_____
AUTHOR

| DATE | / | / |

RATING ☆ ☆ ☆ ☆ ☆

LENGTH
_____
# of pages

○ NON-FICTION
○ FICTION

I LIKED THE ENDING
⊏ YES ⊐ / ⊏ NO ⊐

I READ THIS BOOK

by myself

with: _____

FAVORITE CHARACTER

66

_____

_____

_____

_____

_____

_____ 99

DRAW YOUR FAVORITE CHARACTER OR SCENE

I WOULD LIKE TO ASK THE AUTHOR...

_____

_____

_____

WOULD RECOMMEND TO A FRIEND? ⊏YES⊐ / ⊏NO⊐

Book Review

BOOK #

audiobook ○
paperback ○
eBook ○

_____
TITLE

_____
AUTHOR

| DATE | / | / |

RATING ☆ ☆ ☆ ☆ ☆

LENGTH
_____
# of pages

○ NON-FICTION
○ FICTION

I LIKED THE ENDING
⊏ YES ⊐ / ⊏ NO ⊐

I READ THIS BOOK

by myself

with: _____

FAVORITE CHARACTER

FAVORITE QUOTES

"

_____

_____

_____

_____

_____

_____   "

DRAW YOUR FAVORITE CHARACTER OR SCENE

I WOULD LIKE TO ASK THE AUTHOR...

_____

_____

_____

WOULD RECOMMEND TO A FRIEND?   ⊏ YES ⊐ / ⊏ NO ⊐

Book Review

BOOK #

audiobook ○
paperback ○
eBook ○

_____
TITLE

_____
AUTHOR

DATE / /

RATING ☆ ☆ ☆ ☆ ☆

LENGTH
_____
# of pages

○ NON-FICTION
○ FICTION

I LIKED THE ENDING
⊏ YES ⊐ / ⊏ NO ⊐

I READ THIS BOOK

☐ by myself

☐ with: _____

FAVORITE CHARACTER

FAVORITE QUOTES

66

_____

_____

_____

_____

_____

_____ 99

DRAW YOUR FAVORITE CHARACTER OR SCENE

I WOULD LIKE TO ASK THE AUTHOR...

_____

_____

_____

WOULD RECOMMEND TO A FRIEND? ⊏ YES ⊐ / ⊏ NO ⊐

Book Review

BOOK #

audiobook ○
paperback ○
eBook ○

_____
TITLE

_____
AUTHOR

DATE _____ / _____ / _____

RATING ☆ ☆ ☆ ☆ ☆

LENGTH
_____
# of pages

○ NON-FICTION
○ FICTION

I LIKED THE ENDING
⊏ YES ⊐ / ⊏ NO ⊐

I READ THIS BOOK

by myself

with: _____

FAVORITE CHARACTER

66

_____

_____

_____

_____

_____

_____   99

DRAW YOUR FAVORITE CHARACTER OR SCENE

I WOULD LIKE TO ASK THE AUTHOR...

_____

_____

_____

WOULD RECOMMEND TO A FRIEND? ☐ YES ☐ / ☐ NO ☐

Book Review

BOOK #

audiobook ○
paperback ○
eBook ○

_____
TITLE

_____
AUTHOR

DATE ___ / ___ / ___

RATING ☆ ☆ ☆ ☆ ☆

LENGTH
_____
# of pages

○ NON-FICTION
○ FICTION

I LIKED THE ENDING
⊏ YES ⊐   /   ⊏ NO ⊐

I READ THIS BOOK

☐ by myself

☐ with: _____

FAVORITE CHARACTER

FAVORITE QUOTES

"

"

DRAW YOUR FAVORITE CHARACTER OR SCENE

I WOULD LIKE TO ASK THE AUTHOR...

WOULD RECOMMEND TO A FRIEND? ⊏ YES ⊐ / ⊏ NO ⊐

Book Review

BOOK #

audiobook ○
paperback ○
eBook ○

_____

TITLE

_____

AUTHOR

DATE ___ / ___ / ___

RATING ☆ ☆ ☆ ☆ ☆

LENGTH
_____
# of pages

○ NON-FICTION
○ FICTION

I LIKED THE ENDING
⊏ YES ⊐ / ⊏ NO ⊐

I READ THIS BOOK

by myself

with: _____

FAVORITE CHARACTER

FAVORITE QUOTES

"

_____

_____

_____

_____

_____

_____

"

DRAW YOUR FAVORITE CHARACTER OR SCENE

I WOULD LIKE TO ASK THE AUTHOR...

_____

_____

_____

WOULD RECOMMEND TO A FRIEND? ⊏ YES ⊐ / ⊏ NO ⊐

Book Review

BOOK #

audiobook ○
paperback ○
eBook ○

_____
TITLE

_____
AUTHOR

| DATE | / | / |

LENGTH
_____
# of pages

RATING ☆ ☆ ☆ ☆ ☆

○ NON-FICTION
○ FICTION

I LIKED THE ENDING
⊏ YES ⊐ / ⊏ NO ⊐

I READ THIS BOOK

by myself

with: _____

FAVORITE CHARACTER

FAVORITE QUOTES

"

_____

_____

_____

_____

_____

_____
"

DRAW YOUR FAVORITE CHARACTER OR SCENE

I WOULD LIKE TO ASK THE AUTHOR...

_____

_____

_____

WOULD RECOMMEND TO A FRIEND? ⊏ YES ⊐ / ⊏ NO ⊐

Book Review

BOOK #

audiobook ○
paperback ○
eBook ○

_____
TITLE

_____
AUTHOR

DATE	/	/

RATING ☆ ☆ ☆ ☆ ☆

LENGTH
_____
# of pages

○ NON-FICTION
○ FICTION

I LIKED THE ENDING
⊏ YES ⊐ / ⊏ NO ⊐

I READ THIS BOOK

☐ by myself

☐ with: _____

FAVORITE CHARACTER

FAVORITE QUOTES

66

_____

_____

_____

_____

_____

_____

99

DRAW YOUR FAVORITE CHARACTER OR SCENE

I WOULD LIKE TO ASK THE AUTHOR...

_____

_____

_____

WOULD RECOMMEND TO A FRIEND? ⊏ YES⊐ / ⊏ NO⊐

Book Review

BOOK #

audiobook ○
paperback ○
eBook ○

_____
TITLE

_____
AUTHOR

DATE   /   /

RATING ☆ ☆ ☆ ☆ ☆

LENGTH
_____
# of pages

○ NON-FICTION
○ FICTION

I LIKED THE ENDING
⊏ YES ⊐   /   ⊏ NO ⊐

I READ THIS BOOK

▨ by myself

▨ with: _____

FAVORITE CHARACTER

66

_____

_____

_____

_____

_____

_____

_____

99

DRAW YOUR FAVORITE CHARACTER OR SCENE

I WOULD LIKE TO ASK THE AUTHOR...

_____

_____

_____

WOULD RECOMMEND TO A FRIEND? ⊏YES⊐ / ⊏NO⊐

Book Review

BOOK #

audiobook ○
paperback ○
eBook ○

_____
TITLE

_____
AUTHOR

DATE   /   /

LENGTH
_____
# of pages

RATING ☆ ☆ ☆ ☆ ☆

○ NON-FICTION
○ FICTION

I LIKED THE ENDING
⊏ YES ⊐   /   ⊏ NO ⊐

I READ THIS BOOK

■ by myself

■ with: _____

FAVORITE CHARACTER

FAVORITE QUOTES

“

_____

_____

_____

_____

_____

_____
”

DRAW YOUR FAVORITE CHARACTER OR SCENE

I WOULD LIKE TO ASK THE AUTHOR...

_____

_____

_____

WOULD RECOMMEND TO A FRIEND? ⊏YES⊐ / ⊏NO⊐

Book Review

BOOK #

audiobook ○
paperback ○
eBook ○

_____
TITLE

_____
AUTHOR

| DATE | / | / |

RATING ☆ ☆ ☆ ☆ ☆

LENGTH
_____
# of pages

○ NON-FICTION
○ FICTION

I LIKED THE ENDING
⊏ YES ⊐ / ⊏ NO ⊐

I READ THIS BOOK

by myself

with: _____

FAVORITE CHARACTER

FAVORITE QUOTES

"
_____

_____

_____

_____

_____

_____
"

DRAW YOUR FAVORITE CHARACTER OR SCENE

I WOULD LIKE TO ASK THE AUTHOR...

_____

_____

_____

_____

WOULD RECOMMEND TO A FRIEND?   ⊏ YES ⊐ / ⊏ NO ⊐

Book Review

BOOK #

audiobook ○
paperback ○
eBook ○

_____

TITLE

_____

AUTHOR

| DATE | / | / |

RATING ☆ ☆ ☆ ☆ ☆

LENGTH
_____
# of pages

○ NON-FICTION
○ FICTION

I LIKED THE ENDING
⊏ YES ⊐ / ⊏ NO ⊐

I READ THIS BOOK

by myself

with: _____

FAVORITE CHARACTER

FAVORITE QUOTES

"

_____

_____

_____

_____

_____

_____ "

DRAW YOUR FAVORITE CHARACTER OR SCENE

I WOULD LIKE TO ASK THE AUTHOR...

_____

_____

_____

WOULD RECOMMEND TO A FRIEND? ⊏YES⊐ / ⊏NO⊐

Book Review

BOOK #

audiobook ○
paperback ○
eBook ○

_____
TITLE

_____
AUTHOR

| DATE | / | / |

RATING ☆ ☆ ☆ ☆ ☆

LENGTH
_____
# of pages

○ NON-FICTION
○ FICTION

I READ THIS BOOK

▢ by myself

▢ with: _____

I LIKED THE ENDING
⊏ YES ⊐   /   ⊏ NO ⊐

FAVORITE CHARACTER

FAVORITE QUOTES

66

99

DRAW YOUR FAVORITE CHARACTER OR SCENE

I WOULD LIKE TO ASK THE AUTHOR...

WOULD RECOMMEND TO A FRIEND? ⊏ YES ⊐ / ⊏ NO ⊐

Book Review

BOOK #

audiobook ○
paperback ○
eBook ○

_____
TITLE

_____
AUTHOR

DATE   /   /

RATING ☆ ☆ ☆ ☆ ☆

LENGTH
_____
# of pages

○ NON-FICTION
○ FICTION

I LIKED THE ENDING
☐ YES ☐ / ☐ NO ☐

I READ THIS BOOK

▢ by myself

▢ with: _____

FAVORITE CHARACTER

FAVORITE QUOTES

"

_____

_____

_____

_____

_____

_____
                                              "

DRAW YOUR FAVORITE CHARACTER OR SCENE

I WOULD LIKE TO ASK THE AUTHOR...

_____

_____

_____

WOULD RECOMMEND TO A FRIEND? ⊏ YES ⊐ / ⊏ NO ⊐

Book Review

BOOK #

audiobook ○
paperback ○
eBook ○

_____
TITLE

_____
AUTHOR

| DATE | / | / |

RATING ☆ ☆ ☆ ☆ ☆

LENGTH
_____
# of pages

○ NON-FICTION	I READ THIS BOOK
○ FICTION	▢ by myself
I LIKED THE ENDING	▢ with: _____
⊏ YES ⊐ / ⊏ NO ⊐	

FAVORITE CHARACTER

FAVORITE QUOTES

"

_____

_____

_____

_____

_____

_____
"

DRAW YOUR FAVORITE CHARACTER OR SCENE

I WOULD LIKE TO ASK THE AUTHOR...

_____

_____

_____

WOULD RECOMMEND TO A FRIEND? ⊏ YES ⊐ / ⊏ NO ⊐

Book Review

BOOK #

audiobook ○
paperback ○
eBook ○

_____
TITLE

_____
AUTHOR

DATE   /   /

RATING ☆ ☆ ☆ ☆ ☆

LENGTH
_____
# of pages

○ NON-FICTION	I READ THIS BOOK
○ FICTION	
	☐ by myself
I LIKED THE ENDING	☐ with: _____
☐ YES ☐ / ☐ NO ☐	
FAVORITE CHARACTER	

FAVORITE QUOTES

"

_____

_____

_____

_____

_____

_____
"

DRAW YOUR FAVORITE CHARACTER OR SCENE

I WOULD LIKE TO ASK THE AUTHOR...

_____

_____

_____

WOULD RECOMMEND TO A FRIEND? ⊏ YES ⊐ / ⊏ NO ⊐

Book Review

BOOK #

audiobook ○
paperback ○
eBook ○

_____
TITLE

_____
AUTHOR

DATE ___ / ___ / ___

LENGTH
_____
# of pages

RATING ☆ ☆ ☆ ☆ ☆

○ NON-FICTION
○ FICTION

I READ THIS BOOK

by myself

with: _____

I LIKED THE ENDING
⊏ YES ⊐ / ⊏ NO ⊐

FAVORITE CHARACTER

FAVORITE QUOTES

"
_____

_____

_____

_____

_____

_____
"

DRAW YOUR FAVORITE CHARACTER OR SCENE

I WOULD LIKE TO ASK THE AUTHOR...

_____

_____

_____

WOULD RECOMMEND TO A FRIEND? ☐ YES ☐ / ☐ NO ☐

Book Review

BOOK #

audiobook ◯
paperback ◯
eBook ◯

_____
TITLE

_____
AUTHOR

DATE _____ / _____ / _____

RATING ☆ ☆ ☆ ☆ ☆

LENGTH
_____
# of pages

◯ NON-FICTION
◯ FICTION

I READ THIS BOOK

by myself

with: _____

I LIKED THE ENDING

⊏ YES ⊐   /   ⊏ NO ⊐

FAVORITE CHARACTER

"

"

DRAW YOUR FAVORITE CHARACTER OR SCENE

I WOULD LIKE TO ASK THE AUTHOR...

WOULD RECOMMEND TO A FRIEND? ⊏YES⊐ / ⊏NO⊐

Book Review

BOOK #

audiobook ○
paperback ○
eBook ○

_____
TITLE

_____
AUTHOR

| DATE | / | / |

RATING ☆ ☆ ☆ ☆ ☆

LENGTH
# of pages

○ NON-FICTION
○ FICTION

I LIKED THE ENDING
⌐ YES ⌐ / ⌐ NO ⌐

I READ THIS BOOK

☐ by myself

☐ with: _____

FAVORITE CHARACTER

66

_____

_____

_____

_____

_____

_____

99

DRAW YOUR FAVORITE CHARACTER OR SCENE

I WOULD LIKE TO ASK THE AUTHOR...

_____

_____

_____

WOULD RECOMMEND TO A FRIEND? ⊏YES⊐ / ⊏NO⊐

Book Review

BOOK #

audiobook ◯
paperback ◯
eBook ◯

_____
TITLE

_____
AUTHOR

| DATE | / | / |

RATING ☆ ☆ ☆ ☆ ☆

LENGTH
_____
# of pages

◯ NON-FICTION
◯ FICTION

I LIKED THE ENDING
⊏ YES ⊐ / ⊏ NO ⊐

I READ THIS BOOK

▢ by myself

▢ with: _____

FAVORITE CHARACTER

FAVORITE QUOTES

“

”

DRAW YOUR FAVORITE CHARACTER OR SCENE

I WOULD LIKE TO ASK THE AUTHOR...

WOULD RECOMMEND TO A FRIEND? ⊏YES⊐ / ⊏NO⊐

Book Review

BOOK #

audiobook ○
paperback ○
eBook ○

_____
TITLE

_____
AUTHOR

DATE ____ / ____ / ____

RATING ☆ ☆ ☆ ☆ ☆

LENGTH
_____
# of pages

○ NON-FICTION
○ FICTION

I LIKED THE ENDING
⊏ YES ⊐ / ⊏ NO ⊐

I READ THIS BOOK

▢ by myself

▢ with: _____

FAVORITE CHARACTER

FAVORITE QUOTES

66

_____

_____

_____

_____

_____

_____

99

DRAW YOUR FAVORITE CHARACTER OR SCENE

I WOULD LIKE TO ASK THE AUTHOR...

_____

_____

_____

WOULD RECOMMEND TO A FRIEND? ⊏YES⊐ / ⊏NO⊐

Book Review

BOOK #

audiobook ○
paperback ○
eBook ○

_____
TITLE

_____
AUTHOR

| DATE | / | / |

RATING ☆ ☆ ☆ ☆ ☆

LENGTH
_____
# of pages

○ NON-FICTION
○ FICTION

I LIKED THE ENDING
⊏ YES ⊐ / ⊏ NO ⊐

I READ THIS BOOK

▨ by myself

▨ with: _____

FAVORITE CHARACTER

FAVORITE QUOTES

66

_____

_____

_____

_____

_____

_____
99

DRAW YOUR FAVORITE CHARACTER OR SCENE

I WOULD LIKE TO ASK THE AUTHOR...

_____

_____

_____

WOULD RECOMMEND TO A FRIEND? ⊏ YES⊐ / ⊏ NO⊐

Book Review

BOOK #

audiobook ○
paperback ○
eBook ○

_____
TITLE

_____
AUTHOR

DATE ____ / ____ / ____

LENGTH
_____
# of pages

RATING ☆ ☆ ☆ ☆ ☆

○ NON-FICTION
○ FICTION

I READ THIS BOOK

by myself

with: _____

I LIKED THE ENDING
⊏ YES ⊐ / ⊏ NO ⊐

FAVORITE CHARACTER

66 _____

_____

_____

_____

_____

_____ 99

DRAW YOUR FAVORITE CHARACTER OR SCENE

I WOULD LIKE TO ASK THE AUTHOR...

_____

_____

_____

WOULD RECOMMEND TO A FRIEND? ⊏ YES ⊐ / ⊏ NO ⊐

Book Review

BOOK #

audiobook ○
paperback ○
eBook ○

_____
TITLE

_____
AUTHOR

DATE _____ / _____ / _____

RATING ☆ ☆ ☆ ☆ ☆

LENGTH
_____
# of pages

○ NON-FICTION
○ FICTION

I LIKED THE ENDING
⊏ YES ⊐ / ⊏ NO ⊐

I READ THIS BOOK

◻ by myself

◻ with: _____

FAVORITE CHARACTER

FAVORITE QUOTES

66

_____

_____

_____

_____

_____

_____
99

DRAW YOUR FAVORITE CHARACTER OR SCENE

I WOULD LIKE TO ASK THE AUTHOR...

_____

_____

_____

WOULD RECOMMEND TO A FRIEND? ⊏ YES ⊐ / ⊏ NO ⊐

Book Review

BOOK #

audiobook ○
paperback ○
eBook ○

_____
TITLE

_____
AUTHOR

DATE   /   /

RATING ☆ ☆ ☆ ☆ ☆

LENGTH

_____
# of pages

○ NON-FICTION
○ FICTION

I LIKED THE ENDING
⊏ YES ⊐   /   ⊏ NO ⊐

I READ THIS BOOK

☐ by myself

☐ with: _____

FAVORITE CHARACTER

66

_____

_____

_____

_____

_____

_____ 99

DRAW YOUR FAVORITE CHARACTER OR SCENE

I WOULD LIKE TO ASK THE AUTHOR...

_____

_____

_____

_____

WOULD RECOMMEND TO A FRIEND? ⊏ YES ⊐ / ⊏ NO ⊐

Book Review

BOOK #

audiobook ○
paperback ○
eBook ○

_____

TITLE

_____

AUTHOR

DATE   /   /

RATING ☆ ☆ ☆ ☆ ☆

LENGTH

_____
# of pages

○ NON-FICTION
○ FICTION

I LIKED THE ENDING

⊏ YES ⊐   /   ⊏ NO ⊐

I READ THIS BOOK

by myself

with: _____

FAVORITE CHARACTER

FAVORITE QUOTES

66

_____

_____

_____

_____

_____

_____

99

DRAW YOUR FAVORITE CHARACTER OR SCENE

I WOULD LIKE TO ASK THE AUTHOR...

_____

_____

_____

WOULD RECOMMEND TO A FRIEND? ⊏YES⊐ / ⊏NO⊐

Book Review

BOOK #

audiobook ○
paperback ○
eBook ○

_____
TITLE

_____
AUTHOR

DATE ____ / ____ / ____

LENGTH
_____
# of pages

RATING ☆ ☆ ☆ ☆ ☆

○ NON-FICTION ○ FICTION	**I READ THIS BOOK** ☐ by myself ☐ with: _____
I LIKED THE ENDING ☐ YES ☐ / ☐ NO ☐	
FAVORITE CHARACTER	

FAVORITE QUOTES

"

_____

_____

_____

_____

_____
"

DRAW YOUR FAVORITE CHARACTER OR SCENE

I WOULD LIKE TO ASK THE AUTHOR...

_____

_____

_____

WOULD RECOMMEND TO A FRIEND? ⊏ YES ⊐ / ⊏ NO ⊐

Book Review

BOOK #

audiobook ○
paperback ○
eBook ○

_____
TITLE

_____
AUTHOR

| DATE | / | / |

RATING ☆ ☆ ☆ ☆ ☆

LENGTH
_____
# of pages

○ NON-FICTION
○ FICTION

I LIKED THE ENDING
⊏ YES ⊐ / ⊏ NO ⊐

I READ THIS BOOK

by myself

with: _____

FAVORITE CHARACTER

FAVORITE QUOTES

66

_____

_____

_____

_____

_____

_____

99

DRAW YOUR FAVORITE CHARACTER OR SCENE

I WOULD LIKE TO ASK THE AUTHOR...

_____

_____

_____

WOULD RECOMMEND TO A FRIEND? ⊏YES⊐ / ⊏NO⊐

Book Review

BOOK #

audiobook ◯
paperback ◯
eBook ◯

_____
TITLE

_____
AUTHOR

DATE ___ / ___ / ___

RATING ☆ ☆ ☆ ☆ ☆

LENGTH
_____
# of pages

◯ NON-FICTION
◯ FICTION

I LIKED THE ENDING
⊏ YES ⊐ / ⊏ NO ⊐

I READ THIS BOOK

by myself

with: _____

FAVORITE CHARACTER

FAVORITE QUOTES

66

_____

_____

_____

_____

_____

_____

99

DRAW YOUR FAVORITE CHARACTER OR SCENE

I WOULD LIKE TO ASK THE AUTHOR...

_____

_____

_____

WOULD RECOMMEND TO A FRIEND? ⊏ YES ⊐ / ⊏ NO ⊐

Book Review

BOOK #

audiobook ○
paperback ○
eBook ○

_____
TITLE

_____
AUTHOR

DATE ____ / ____ / ____

RATING ☆ ☆ ☆ ☆ ☆

LENGTH
_____
# of pages

○ NON-FICTION
○ FICTION

I LIKED THE ENDING
⊏ YES ⊐ / ⊏ NO ⊐

I READ THIS BOOK

☐ by myself

☐ with: _____

FAVORITE CHARACTER

66

_____

_____

_____

_____

_____

_____

99

DRAW YOUR FAVORITE CHARACTER OR SCENE

I WOULD LIKE TO ASK THE AUTHOR...

_____

_____

_____

WOULD RECOMMEND TO A FRIEND? ⊏ YES ⊐ / ⊏ NO ⊐

Book Review

BOOK #

audiobook ○
paperback ○
eBook ○

_____
TITLE

_____
AUTHOR

DATE   /   /

LENGTH
_____
# of pages

RATING ☆ ☆ ☆ ☆ ☆

○ NON-FICTION
○ FICTION

I LIKED THE ENDING
⊏ YES ⊐   /   ⊏ NO ⊐

I READ THIS BOOK

by myself

with: _____

FAVORITE CHARACTER

FAVORITE QUOTES

66

_____

_____

_____

_____

_____

_____ 99

DRAW YOUR FAVORITE CHARACTER OR SCENE

I WOULD LIKE TO ASK THE AUTHOR...

_____

_____

_____

WOULD RECOMMEND TO A FRIEND? ⊏YES⊐ / ⊏NO⊐

Book Review

BOOK #

audiobook ○
paperback ○
eBook ○

_____

TITLE

_____

AUTHOR

| DATE | / | / |

LENGTH

# of pages

RATING ☆ ☆ ☆ ☆ ☆

○ NON-FICTION ○ FICTION	I READ THIS BOOK
I LIKED THE ENDING ⊏ YES ⊐ / ⊏ NO ⊐	☐ by myself ☐ with: _____
FAVORITE CHARACTER	

FAVORITE QUOTES

66

_____

_____

_____

_____

_____

_____
99

DRAW YOUR FAVORITE CHARACTER OR SCENE

I WOULD LIKE TO ASK THE AUTHOR...

_____

_____

_____

WOULD RECOMMEND TO A FRIEND?   ⊏ YES ⊐ / ⊏ NO ⊐

Book Review

BOOK #

audiobook ○
paperback ○
eBook ○

_____

TITLE

_____

AUTHOR

DATE _____ / _____ / _____

RATING ☆ ☆ ☆ ☆ ☆

LENGTH

_____
# of pages

○ NON-FICTION
○ FICTION

I READ THIS BOOK

▢ by myself

▢ with: _____

I LIKED THE ENDING

▢ YES ▢ / ▢ NO ▢

FAVORITE CHARACTER

FAVORITE QUOTES

66

_____

_____

_____

_____

_____

_____

99

DRAW YOUR FAVORITE CHARACTER OR SCENE

I WOULD LIKE TO ASK THE AUTHOR...

_____

_____

_____

_____

WOULD RECOMMEND TO A FRIEND? ⊏YES⊐ / ⊏NO⊐

Book Review

BOOK #

audiobook ○
paperback ○
eBook ○

_____
TITLE

_____
AUTHOR

| DATE | / | / |

RATING ☆ ☆ ☆ ☆ ☆

LENGTH
_____
# of pages

○ NON-FICTION
○ FICTION

I LIKED THE ENDING
⊏ YES ⊐ / ⊏ NO ⊐

I READ THIS BOOK

▢ by myself

▢ with: _____

FAVORITE CHARACTER

FAVORITE QUOTES

"

_____

_____

_____

_____

_____

_____

"

DRAW YOUR FAVORITE CHARACTER OR SCENE

I WOULD LIKE TO ASK THE AUTHOR...

_____

_____

_____

WOULD RECOMMEND TO A FRIEND? ☐ YES ☐ / ☐ NO ☐

Book Review

BOOK #

audiobook ○
paperback ○
eBook ○

_____

TITLE

_____

AUTHOR

| DATE | / | / |

RATING ☆ ☆ ☆ ☆ ☆

LENGTH

_____
# of pages

○ NON-FICTION
○ FICTION

I LIKED THE ENDING
☐ YES ☐ / ☐ NO ☐

I READ THIS BOOK

by myself

with: _____

FAVORITE CHARACTER

" "

WOULD RECOMMEND TO A FRIEND? ⊏ YES ⊐ / ⊏ NO ⊐

Book Review

BOOK #

audiobook ○
paperback ○
eBook ○

_____
TITLE

_____
AUTHOR

DATE   /   /

RATING ☆ ☆ ☆ ☆ ☆

LENGTH

_____
# of pages

○ NON-FICTION
○ FICTION

I LIKED THE ENDING
⌐ YES ⌐   /   ⌐ NO ⌐

I READ THIS BOOK

by myself

with: _____

FAVORITE CHARACTER

FAVORITE QUOTES

"

_____

_____

_____

_____

_____

_____
"

DRAW YOUR FAVORITE CHARACTER OR SCENE

I WOULD LIKE TO ASK THE AUTHOR...

_____

_____

_____

WOULD RECOMMEND TO A FRIEND? ⊏ YES ⊐ / ⊏ NO ⊐

Book Review

BOOK #

audiobook ○
paperback ○
eBook ○

_____
TITLE

_____
AUTHOR

DATE ___ / ___ / ___

RATING ☆ ☆ ☆ ☆ ☆

LENGTH
_____
# of pages

○ NON-FICTION ○ FICTION	I READ THIS BOOK
I LIKED THE ENDING ⊏ YES ⊐ / ⊏ NO ⊐	▢ by myself ▢ with: _____

FAVORITE CHARACTER

FAVORITE QUOTES

66

_____

_____

_____

_____

_____

_____
99

DRAW YOUR FAVORITE CHARACTER OR SCENE

I WOULD LIKE TO ASK THE AUTHOR...

_____

_____

_____

WOULD RECOMMEND TO A FRIEND? ⊏YES⊐ / ⊏NO⊐

Book Review

BOOK #

audiobook ○
paperback ○
eBook ○

_____
TITLE

_____
AUTHOR

| DATE | / | / |

LENGTH
_____
# of pages

RATING ☆ ☆ ☆ ☆ ☆

○ NON-FICTION
○ FICTION

I LIKED THE ENDING
⊏ YES ⊐ / ⊏ NO ⊐

I READ THIS BOOK

by myself

with: _____

FAVORITE CHARACTER

FAVORITE QUOTES

" _____

_____

_____

_____

_____

_____ "

DRAW YOUR FAVORITE CHARACTER OR SCENE

I WOULD LIKE TO ASK THE AUTHOR...

_____

_____

_____

WOULD RECOMMEND TO A FRIEND?   ⊏YES⊐ / ⊏NO⊐

Book Review

BOOK #

audiobook ○
paperback ○
eBook ○

_____
TITLE

_____
AUTHOR

DATE ____ / ____ / ____

LENGTH

_____
# of pages

RATING ☆ ☆ ☆ ☆ ☆

○ NON-FICTION
○ FICTION

I LIKED THE ENDING
⊏ YES ⊐   /   ⊏ NO ⊐

I READ THIS BOOK

☐ by myself

☐ with: _____

FAVORITE CHARACTER

FAVORITE QUOTES

66

_____

_____

_____

_____

_____

_____

99

DRAW YOUR FAVORITE CHARACTER OR SCENE

I WOULD LIKE TO ASK THE AUTHOR...

_____

_____

_____

WOULD RECOMMEND TO A FRIEND? ⊏YES⊐ / ⊏NO⊐

Book Review

BOOK #

audiobook ○
paperback ○
eBook ○

_____
TITLE

_____
AUTHOR

| DATE | / | / |

RATING ☆ ☆ ☆ ☆ ☆

LENGTH
_____
# of pages

○ NON-FICTION
○ FICTION

I LIKED THE ENDING
⊏ YES ⊐ / ⊏ NO ⊐

I READ THIS BOOK

by myself

with: _____

FAVORITE CHARACTER

FAVORITE QUOTES

"

"

DRAW YOUR FAVORITE CHARACTER OR SCENE

I WOULD LIKE TO ASK THE AUTHOR...

WOULD RECOMMEND TO A FRIEND?   ⊏YES⊐ / ⊏NO⊐

Book Review

BOOK #

audiobook ○
paperback ○
eBook ○

_____
TITLE

_____
AUTHOR

DATE ___ / ___ / ___

LENGTH
_____
# of pages

RATING ☆ ☆ ☆ ☆ ☆

○ NON-FICTION
○ FICTION

I LIKED THE ENDING
⊏ YES ⊐ / ⊏ NO ⊐

I READ THIS BOOK

by myself

with: _____

FAVORITE CHARACTER

FAVORITE QUOTES

66

_____

_____

_____

_____

_____

_____

99

DRAW YOUR FAVORITE CHARACTER OR SCENE

I WOULD LIKE TO ASK THE AUTHOR...

_____

_____

_____

WOULD RECOMMEND TO A FRIEND? ☐ YES☐ / ☐ NO☐

Book Review

BOOK #

audiobook ○
paperback ○
eBook ○

_____
TITLE

_____
AUTHOR

DATE   /   /

RATING ☆ ☆ ☆ ☆ ☆

LENGTH
_____
# of pages

○ NON-FICTION
○ FICTION

I LIKED THE ENDING
⊏ YES ⊐   /   ⊏ NO ⊐

I READ THIS BOOK

☐ by myself

☐ with: _____

FAVORITE CHARACTER

" _____

_____

_____

_____

_____

_____ "

DRAW YOUR FAVORITE CHARACTER OR SCENE

I WOULD LIKE TO ASK THE AUTHOR...

_____

_____

_____

WOULD RECOMMEND TO A FRIEND? ☐ YES ☐ / ☐ NO ☐

Book Review

BOOK #

audiobook ○
paperback ○
eBook ○

_____
TITLE

_____
AUTHOR

DATE _____ / _____ / _____

RATING ☆ ☆ ☆ ☆ ☆

LENGTH
_____
# of pages

○ NON-FICTION
○ FICTION

I LIKED THE ENDING
⊏ YES ⊐ / ⊏ NO ⊐

I READ THIS BOOK

by myself

with: _____

FAVORITE CHARACTER

FAVORITE QUOTES

66

"

DRAW YOUR FAVORITE CHARACTER OR SCENE

I WOULD LIKE TO ASK THE AUTHOR...

WOULD RECOMMEND TO A FRIEND? ⊏ YES ⊐ / ⊏ NO ⊐

Book Review

BOOK #

audiobook ○
paperback ○
eBook ○

_____
TITLE

_____
AUTHOR

DATE ___ / ___ / ___

RATING ☆ ☆ ☆ ☆ ☆

LENGTH
_____
# of pages

○ NON-FICTION
○ FICTION

I READ THIS BOOK

▢ by myself

▢ with: _____

I LIKED THE ENDING
⊏ YES ⊐ / ⊏ NO ⊐

FAVORITE CHARACTER

FAVORITE QUOTES

❝

_____

_____

_____

_____

_____

_____
❞

DRAW YOUR FAVORITE CHARACTER OR SCENE

I WOULD LIKE TO ASK THE AUTHOR...

_____

_____

_____

WOULD RECOMMEND TO A FRIEND? ⊏YES⊐ / ⊏NO⊐

Book Review

BOOK #

audiobook ○
paperback ○
eBook ○

_____
TITLE

_____
AUTHOR

DATE   /   /

RATING ☆ ☆ ☆ ☆ ☆

LENGTH
# of pages

○ NON-FICTION
○ FICTION

I LIKED THE ENDING
⊏ YES ⊐   /   ⊏ NO ⊐

I READ THIS BOOK

by myself

with: _____

FAVORITE CHARACTER

FAVORITE QUOTES

66

_____

_____

_____

_____

_____

_____

99

DRAW YOUR FAVORITE CHARACTER OR SCENE

I WOULD LIKE TO ASK THE AUTHOR...

_____

_____

_____

WOULD RECOMMEND TO A FRIEND?   ☐ YES☐ / ☐ NO☐

Book Review

BOOK #

audiobook ○
paperback ○
eBook ○

_____
TITLE

_____
AUTHOR

DATE _____ / _____ / _____

LENGTH
_____
# of pages

RATING ☆ ☆ ☆ ☆ ☆

○ NON-FICTION
○ FICTION

I READ THIS BOOK

▢ by myself

▢ with: _____

I LIKED THE ENDING
⊏ YES ⊐ / ⊏ NO ⊐

FAVORITE CHARACTER

FAVORITE QUOTES

66

_____

_____

_____

_____

_____

_____

99

DRAW YOUR FAVORITE CHARACTER OR SCENE

I WOULD LIKE TO ASK THE AUTHOR...

_____

_____

_____

WOULD RECOMMEND TO A FRIEND? ⊏ YES⊐ / ⊏ NO⊐

Book Review

BOOK #

audiobook ○
paperback ○
eBook ○

_____
TITLE

_____
AUTHOR

DATE   /   /

RATING ☆ ☆ ☆ ☆ ☆

LENGTH

# of pages

○ NON-FICTION
○ FICTION

I LIKED THE ENDING
⊏ YES ⊐   /   ⊏ NO ⊐

I READ THIS BOOK

by myself

with: _____

FAVORITE CHARACTER

FAVORITE QUOTES

66

_____

_____

_____

_____

_____

_____

99

DRAW YOUR FAVORITE CHARACTER OR SCENE

I WOULD LIKE TO ASK THE AUTHOR...

_____

_____

_____

WOULD RECOMMEND TO A FRIEND? ⊏ YES ⊐ / ⊏ NO ⊐

Book Review

BOOK #

audiobook ○
paperback ○
eBook ○

_____
TITLE

_____
AUTHOR

DATE _____ / _____ / _____

RATING ☆ ☆ ☆ ☆ ☆

LENGTH
_____
# of pages

○ NON-FICTION	I READ THIS BOOK
○ FICTION	
	▢ by myself
I LIKED THE ENDING	▢ with: _____
⊏ YES ⊐ / ⊏ NO ⊐	

FAVORITE CHARACTER

FAVORITE QUOTES

"

_____

_____

_____

_____

_____

_____   "

DRAW YOUR FAVORITE CHARACTER OR SCENE

I WOULD LIKE TO ASK THE AUTHOR...

_____

_____

_____

WOULD RECOMMEND TO A FRIEND? ⊏ YES ⊐ / ⊏ NO ⊐

Book Review

BOOK #

audiobook ◯
paperback ◯
eBook ◯

_____
TITLE

_____
AUTHOR

DATE   /   /

RATING ☆ ☆ ☆ ☆ ☆

LENGTH
_____
# of pages

◯ NON-FICTION
◯ FICTION

I LIKED THE ENDING
⊏ YES ⊐   /   ⊏ NO ⊐

I READ THIS BOOK

by myself

with: _____

FAVORITE CHARACTER

FAVORITE QUOTES

"

"

DRAW YOUR FAVORITE CHARACTER OR SCENE

I WOULD LIKE TO ASK THE AUTHOR...

WOULD RECOMMEND TO A FRIEND? ⊏ YES ⊐ / ⊏ NO ⊐

Book Review

BOOK #

audiobook ○
paperback ○
eBook ○

_____
TITLE

_____
AUTHOR

| DATE | / | / |

LENGTH
_____
# of pages

RATING ☆ ☆ ☆ ☆ ☆

○ NON-FICTION
○ FICTION

I LIKED THE ENDING
⊏ YES ⊐ / ⊏ NO ⊐

I READ THIS BOOK

◻ by myself

◻ with: _____

FAVORITE CHARACTER

FAVORITE QUOTES

"

_____

_____

_____

_____

_____

_____   "

DRAW YOUR FAVORITE CHARACTER OR SCENE

I WOULD LIKE TO ASK THE AUTHOR...

_____

_____

_____

WOULD RECOMMEND TO A FRIEND? ⊏ YES ⊐ / ⊏ NO ⊐

Book Review

BOOK #

audiobook ○
paperback ○
eBook ○

_____
TITLE

_____
AUTHOR

DATE _____ / _____ / _____

RATING ☆ ☆ ☆ ☆ ☆

LENGTH
_____
# of pages

○ NON-FICTION
○ FICTION

I LIKED THE ENDING
⊏ YES ⊐ / ⊏ NO ⊐

I READ THIS BOOK

by myself

with: _____

FAVORITE CHARACTER

FAVORITE QUOTES

66

_____

_____

_____

_____

_____

_____   99

DRAW YOUR FAVORITE CHARACTER OR SCENE

I WOULD LIKE TO ASK THE AUTHOR...

_____

_____

_____

WOULD RECOMMEND TO A FRIEND? ⊏ YES⊐ / ⊏ NO⊐

Well done! 52 books down
and and so many more await!

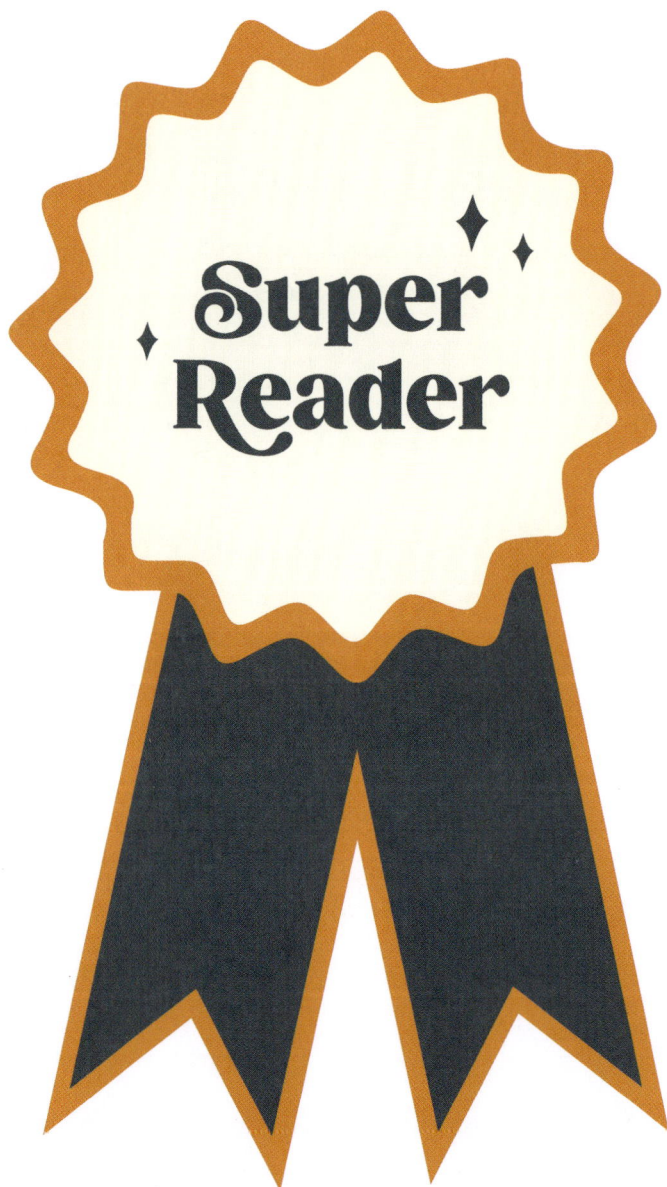

Super
Reader